THE PATH OF EVERY MAN

...WHO FOLLOWS AFTER THE HEART OF GOD

Requests for information should be addressed to:
1% Publishing
8500 Teel Parkway
Frisco, TX, 75034
214-387-9833
www.elevatelife.com

Book Layout/Design: 1% Publishing

Printed in the United States of America.

ISBN: 979-8-9874069-5-3 (Paperback/Leader's Guide)
ISBN: 979-8-9874069-6-0 (Paperback/Workbook)

Printed in the United States of America

Table of Contents

SESSION 1: Introduction 7

SESSION 2: The Path of a Son 13

SESSION 3: The Path of a Servant 27

SESSION 4: The Path of a Friend 43

SESSION 5: The Path of a Lover 61

SESSION 6: The Path of a Warrior 83

SESSION 7: The Path of a King 99

SESSION 8: The Path of a Father 115

HOW THIS STUDY WORKS

WELCOME

In life, men can follow a variety of paths.

Most choose their path by default, rather than by design. This study examines the life of David – a man after God's own heart. It reveals a path we can choose to follow ... a Think, Be, Do path to living by design ... "The Path of Every Man ... who follows after the Heart of God."

> *"Show me the right path, O Lord;*
> *point out the road to follow.*
> *Lead me by your truth and teach me,*
> *for you are the God who saves me.*
> *All day long I put my hope in you"*
> **Psalm 25:4,5**

We are excited you have joined us as we embark on this journey!

THE STUDY

We put a lot of thought and prayer into the flow and content of this study. Together, the Videos and Workbook create an in-depth, interactive experience for you – whether individually or in a group. ***(Video link can be found at the end of this book.)***

This is an eight-session study, comprised of an introduction and seven paths. You will complete one path each time you meet. The paths are comprised of three, 10-minute video segments covering the THINK, BE, and DO of each path.

> Note: The THINK, BE, and DO flow of each path is strategic and intentional. Here is why ... we each have a philosophy of life. This philosophy is a reflection of how we Think, Be, and Do life. Our Think, plus our Be, plus our Do, determines what we HAVE in life ... success or failure. Most men live life by default, rather than design, as they did not have a Think, Be, Do path to follow. Instead, they forged their own path. This study introduces you to a path that will give a "God design" to your life, so that you do not live by default. The THINK, BE, and DO flow is explained in the introduction video segment.

You will begin each session by watching the THINK video segment. Follow the Video Outline provided in the workbook. Then review the Key Points, Discussion Questions, and Pray. Follow this pattern for the Think, Be, Do segments for each path. Overall, sessions will last approximately 60 to 90 minutes, depending upon group size and depth of discussions.

<u>THE WORKBOOK</u>

This workbook provides:

- **Content Outlines** – for the group to follow when watching the video segments

- **Scripture References** – to denote all scriptures cited in the video segments

- **Key Thoughts** – to highlight the main points introduced in the video segments

- **Discussion Questions** – to facilitate group discussions

- **Prayers** – for group prayer

- **Notes Pages** – for capturing personal thoughts, insights, and action items

SESSION 1

INTRODUCTION
THE PATH OF EVERY MAN

SESSION 1
INTRODUCTION

 VIDEO

Psalm 25:1-15 NLT
Proverbs 20:6

1. THE PATH OF A _____Son_____ LIFE LESSON: _____Honor_____

2. THE PATH OF A _____Servant_____ LIFE LESSON: _____Fellowship that breeds leadership_____

3. THE PATH OF A _____Friend_____ LIFE LESSON: _____Faithfulness/Loyalty_____

4. THE PATH OF A _____Lover_____ LIFE LESSON: _____Excellence_____

5. THE PATH OF A _____Warrior_____ LIFE LESSON: _____Fight/Conflict Resolution_____

Genesis 1:26-28

6. THE PATH OF A _____King_____ LIFE LESSON: _____Rule_____

7. THE PATH OF A _____Father_____ LIFE LESSON: _____Legacy_____

2 Chronicles 16:9

NOTES

🔑 KEY THOUGHTS

In life, men can follow a variety of paths. Most choose their path by default, rather than by design. This study examines the life of David – a man after God's own heart. It reveals a path we can choose to follow ... a Think, Be, Do path to living by design, "The Path of Every Man ... who follows after the Heart of God."

💬 DISCUSSION

? Discuss what you most want to get out of this study.

☝ PRAYER

Father, thank you for this study. Please prepare our ears to hear and our hearts to receive. Lead us by your truth and teach us what we need to know to be men that follow after Your heart. In Jesus name, Amen.

NOTES

NOTES ————

SESSION 2
THE PATH OF A SON

Part 1: The "THINK" of a Son

 VIDEO

Acts 13:22; Psalm 25:1-14

1. THINK _____Obedience_____

Romans 8:12-17

- As a son, you Think Obedience by "FIRST" thinking about your Father's Business.

1 Samuel 16:11

BENEFITS OF OBEDIENCE

- God is able to prove His goodness *(Deuteronomy 7:9)*

- You Will REAL-ize your True Value *(Exodus 19:5)*

- God's hand will be upon you *(Ephesians 6:1,2)*

NOTES

LIFE LESSON: _____Honor_____

🔑 KEY THOUGHTS

We are all born sons but we have to learn what it means to be a son of God.

Acts 13:22 sets the stage for showing David's heart – David was a son of Jesse but also a son of God. David did not do some of God's will, he did all of God's will. David's heart was to learn God's ways and do what God wanted him to do. God saw his heart.

A son **THINKS** "Obedience." Obedience does not come naturally. Rather, to most, "doing what I want" comes naturally.

Learning obedience begins with THINKing first about your father's business. The story of Jesus, when separated from His parents at the age of 12, shows the revelation He had that everything He did was about His Father's business.

Three benefits of obedience are:

- **God is able to prove His goodness.** *(Deuteronomy 7:9)* God wants to prove His "God-ness" … he wants to prove His goodness.

- **You real-ize your true value.** *(Exodus 19:5)* When you obey God and He proves His goodness, you begin to realize you have value with Him … to Him you are a special treasure.

- **His hand comes upon us in a big way.** *(Ephesians 6:1-2)* Learning to honor your parents is

NOTES

where it is supposed to begin. Learning to honor begins with learning obedience.

💬 DISCUSSION

? As you watched this session, where did you find your heart and mind going? What stood out to you?

? In what ways can you be more about your Father's business?

? What are some areas in your life where you need to become more obedient?

☝ PRAYER

Father, show me your path. Teach me your way. I want to do what you want me to do, not what I would do. I want to have a heart like David. Help me to first Think about your business. Help me to Think obedience so that I may learn the lesson of a son, which is honor. In Jesus name, Amen.

NOTES

NOTES ——————————————

SESSION 2
THE PATH OF A SON

Part 2: The "BE" of a Son

 VIDEO

LIFE LESSON: HONOR

1. **THINK OBEDIENCE**

2. **BE A PART OF THE** _____Family_____ _____Values_____

   • Sons of Origin/Son of Choice *(1 Corinthians 4:15)*

   • Sons make important to them what is important to the father.

   • Sons develop a teachable spirit. *(Hebrews 12:5-17)*

   • Sons learn the discipline of small things. (Bears, Lions, Giants)

NOTES

18

🔑 KEY THOUGHTS

When you **THINK** obedience, you can **BE** part of the Family Values. Values are what matter most. This was the secret of David having a heart that followed after the heart God. David tapped into what was important to God and made that important to him. Many things can be important in life. Your career, house, and car are all important, but they are all superficial. What is really important is what God says is important.

We must place value on the family values to be part of the family business. Jesus was part of the family business. To be part of what He did and what David was all about, we must be part of the family values and choose to be a son of choice.

Being part of the family values necessitates:

- Understanding that you are a son of choice. God chose you. You did not choose Him. He chose you before you formed in your mother's womb. *(1 Corinthians 4:15)*

- Making important to you what is important to the Father. Have the kind of heart that says, "Show me Your way, not mine."

- Developing a teachable spirit. Hearing the voices of fathers. You will have many teachers but few fathers. Identify the father voices in your life. The world calls this mentorship. But in this context, it is way more than that – it is having a voice that speaks to who you are as a son of God. *(Hebrews 12:5-13)*

- Learning the discipline of the small things.

NOTES

The "Be" of the son is for us to know that we are part of the family values. Be sons of choice, sons that value what God says to value, sons that are teachable and sons that learn the discipline in small things.

🗩 DISCUSSION

? How can you make what is important to God important to you?

? Who are some of the father voices in your life? If you need a father voice in a particular area, what is a step you can take toward identifying that person.

? What is one little thing in which you need to be more disciplined? What is on step you can take toward that?

☝ PRAYER

Father, I choose to be your son and want to be part of the family values. I want to make what is important to you, important to me. Please help me to have a teachable spirit and to respond positively with the correction I receive from your Word. Help me to be disciplined in the little things so the big things will take care of themselves. In Your name, Amen.

NOTES

NOTES

THE PATH OF A SON

Part 3: The "DO" of a Son

▶ VIDEO

1. **THINK OBEDIENCE**

   Psalm 25:8,9

2. **BE A PART OF THE FAMILY VALUES**

   • Sons learn the discipline of small things. (Bears, Lions, Giants)

3. **DO** ___Self___ ___Mastery___

   ❝ *Self-Discipline opens the door to Self-Discovery which breeds Self-Confidence which develops Self-Competence = Self-Mastery!"* // **Leadershipology.com**

   ### LIFE LESSON: HONOR

   ❝ *The path of a son is to teach a man to be able to master honor, so that he will HAVE honor."* // **Leadershipology.com**

NOTES

22

🔑 KEY THOUGHTS

The **DO** of a son is self-mastery. Developing self-mastery begins with self-discipline. Self-discipline opens the door to Self-discovery which breeds Self-confidence which develops Self-Competence = Self-Mastery.

The defeats experienced by David were personal defeats (i.e., Bathsheba, Uriah). They stemmed from self-mastery issues. When you can be faithful in the little things, you are getting self-mastery. Although we have passed tests related to obedience and honor, it does not mean the next test is going to be easy just because we had passed others before.

If your father of origin did not "live the life," you need to find a father voice in your life. You can honor your father of origin because he brought you into this world, but you do need to find fathers you can honor that will speak into your life.

God wants us to understand that self-mastery begins when we think obedience, Be Part of the Family Values, Do Self-Mastery in giving honor to Him and those voices that He wants to use in my life to help me on the path of the son.

NOTES

🗨 DISCUSSION

? Think about a personal defeat or failure you have faced. Was it related to a self-mastery issue? What can you be more disciplined in to keep you from facing a similar defeat in the future?

? What area(s) in life do you need a father voice? Financial? Marriage? Career? Health? Spiritual walk? Other?

☝ PRAYER

Father, help me to be obedient, to Be part of the family values, and to Do self-mastery. I want your way, not mine. I want to honor you and the voices You want to use in my life to help me on the path of the son. Please align me with the right people, in the right place, at the right time, so that the right things can happen in my life. In Jesus name, Amen.

NOTES

NOTES

25

SESSION 3

THE PATH OF A SERVANT
LIFE LESSON: FOLLOW-SHIP
THAT BREEDS LEADERSHIP

SESSION 3
THE PATH OF A SERVANT

Part 1: The "THINK" of a Servant

 VIDEO

Psalm 78:70-72
1 Samuel 16:11-12
Psalm 89:20-24
Matthew 20:26-28

1. **THINK** _____Noble_____

- Noble – *one who because of elevation of mind, become heroic by doing deeds "uncommonly" well with excellence as the standard.*

- Nobility requires a standard of excellence. To be noble literally means *"greatness of soul."*

LIFE LESSON: _____**FOLLOW-SHIP THAT BREEDS LEADERSHIP**_____

NOTES

FIVE NOBLE WAYS OF THINKING

- Think **N** ____eedfully____ *(John 6:1-14)*

- Think **O** ____pportunistically____ *(Exodus 19:5)*

> ❝*Opportunities of a lifetime must be seized in the lifetime of the opportunity."* **// Leonard Revenhill**

- Think **B** ____ountifully____ *(Ephesians 6:1,2)*

> ❝*The world of the generous gets larger and larger; the world of the stingy, gets smaller and smaller."* **// Proverbs 11:24 (MSG)**

- Think **L** ____ittle becomes much____ becomes much when handled faithfully

> ❝*It is being mindful of the little things that develops a spirit of excellence and sharpens your 1%."* **// Your Divine Fingerprint, p.112**

- Think **E** ____ternally____ *(John 6:14, Matthew 16:24-27; Philippians 2:5-11)*

NOTES ──

KEY THOUGHTS

As servants of God, He causes us to have integrity of heart, to say what we mean and mean what we say, and to lead our lives and others with the skillfulness of our hands. (Psalm 78:70-72)

Servants **THINK** NOBLE.

Noble defined is, *"One who because of elevation of mind, becomes heroic by doing deeds 'uncommonly' well with excellence as the standard."* As a Servant, that is your job. Become heroic, not because you are trying to be a hero, but because of elevation of mind and doing common deeds uncommonly well with a spirit of excellence.

Nobility requires a standard of excellence. To be noble literally means "greatness of soul." So, Think NOBLE.

Revisit the five NOBLE ways of Thinking outlined above.

As a Servant, when we Think NOBLE we are saying, "Here's a need. Here's an opportunity for me to be bountiful, to take the little that I have and to handle it faithfully." When we have that spirit and that heart, God's hand comes upon us in a powerful, powerful way.

NOTES

💬 DISCUSSION

? Nobility requires a spirit of excellence. What is an area in your life where you consistently exhibited a spirit of excellence?

? Is there an area where in life where you have not been consistently excellent?

? Do you Think Needfully? In essence, do you see the needs of others and serve them? Share some examples.

☝ PRAYER

Father, I want to be a servant and Think NOBLE. Help me to see the needs of others, to seize opportunities for me to be bountiful and take the little that I have and handle it faithfully. In Jesus name, Amen.

NOTES

SESSION 3
THE PATH OF A SERVANT

Part 2: The "BE" of a Servant

 VIDEO

LIFE LESSON: FOLLOW-SHIP THAT BREEDS LEADERSHIP

1. **THINK NOBLE**

2. **BE** _____Humble_____

Philippians 2:5-16 NIV

• Servants develop _____Humility_____

Huperetes: *an under rower.*

Does not dictate his own course of action but yields to another authority for the sake of accomplishing a specific task.

Under rowers worked together at the command of a supervisor to move a mighty ship through the water.

NOTES

33

- Servants demonstrate _____ Honor _____

> **Diakonos:** *to hasten after or pursue; to give honor*
>
> - Give honor through follow-ship
>
> - Give honor by serving with the best interests of others in mind

KEY THOUGHTS

Servants **BE** Humble.

There is no greater quality that any man can have than to be humble, to choose to give up his right to be right. This is what Jesus modeled. This is what David modeled when he went to fight Goliath. David's heart, even with Goliath, was not to score a victory. It was not even to look good to the king.

Servants develop humility. The word bond-servant in the Greek is "huperetes," which means under rower. God wants us to have the picture of humbling ourselves as under rower to make the Kingdom of God advance, to make what God has put you on the earth to be about what He is doing, not what I'm doing or want.

Throughout scripture, humility precedes honor. In the book of Proverbs, it says that by humility and fear (honor) of the Lord come riches, honor, and life. So, by giving up our right to be right, taking the form of a servant, and choosing to give honor, come riches, honor, and life.

NOTES

Be a servant who chooses to humble himself to give honor. Be one who gives honor by serving with the best interest of others in mind. In doing this, God opens the windows of heaven over your life where He can flow riches honor, and life – quality life – back into your life.

💬 DISCUSSION

? Think about your heart … why do you do what you do? Why do you do what you do for your wife? For your kids? On your job?

? Share a time when it was challenging for you to give up you right to be right. What makes it difficult?

? Share a time when you gave up your right to be right. What affect did that have on the relationship you have with that person?

☝ PRAYER

Father, help me to be a servant who chooses to humble himself to give honor. One who gives honor by serving with the best interest of others in mind. In Jesus name, Amen.

NOTES

THE PATH OF A SERVANT

Part 3: The "DO" of a Servant

📽 VIDEO

1. **THINK NOBLE**

2. **BE HUMBLE**

3. **DO** _____Greatness_____

LIFE LESSON: FOLLOW-SHIP THAT BREEDS LEADERSHIP

Luke 9:46-48
Matthew 23:11-12
Matthew 20:20-28
1 Corinthians 4:1-2

THE THREE-STRANDED CORD OF GREATNESS

1. _____Servant_____

NOTES ────────────────────────────────

> **"***A servant-leader is someone who is called by God with others to be great. The willingly come under spiritual authority with the attitude of serving others. They have a passion for excellence and a desire to lead. The choose to take the form of a "slave," to be one whose will is swallowed up in the will of another. They become a living sacrifice whereby their "sacred" life dispels all mediocrity."* // **Leadershipology.com**

> **"***Everybody can be great … because anybody can serve. You don't have to have a college degree to serve. You don't have to make your subject and verb agree to serve. You only need a heart full of grace. A soul generated by love."* // **Martin Luther King, Jr.**

2.   _____ Steward _____

Steward: *Gr. oikonomos – a house arranger. It pictures one who oversees and dispenses the property and goods of another. He doesn't own goods of another but is entrusted with their care and charged to be faithful in his duties.*

- Stewards _____ understand _____ everything they have God gave them to oversee for Him.

- Stewards "arrange the house" of God by making _____ possible _____ the impossible (unveil the mysteries of God).

3.   _____ Sowers _____

2 Corinthians 9:6-8, 10-11

38

THE PATH OF A SERVANT

4 GREAT THINGS GREAT SERVANTS DO

- Focus on what you ___have to give___, not on what you want to receive.

- Focus on what's needed, not what ___you need___.

- Focus on what you ___CAN DO___, not on what you CAN'T DO.

- Focus on helping ___others___ get what they want, rather than you getting what you want.

// P115 &116 YDF

KEY THOUGHTS

Servants **THINK** Noble; **BE** Humble; and **DO** Greatness.

The three-stranded cord of Greatness includes:

- **Servant:** A servant leader is someone who is called by God with others to be great. In other words, it's not just about you. Many people are all about serving themselves, their family, their career … and not about serving the Kingdom of God. A servant is one who humbles himself, one who honors. Revisit the definition of a servant-leader above.

- **Steward:** Stewards understand everything they have God gave to them to oversee for Him. Stewards arrange the house of God, making possible the impossible (unveil the mysteries of God) … in essence, for everything that needs to happen in the House of God, stewards arrange for it to happen.

NOTES

- **Sowers:** Review 2 Corinthians 9:6-8. Tithing and sowing are different. Tithing is returning to God the first tenth of your increase. Sowing is what you choose to give beyond the tithe. God wants you to be a cheerful sower. His Word says He gives seed to the sower. He does not give it to those who simply work hard, he gives seed to the sower. Sowers do not ask God what to give. Rather they give as they purpose in their heart. If God can get it through you, He will get it to you.

To Do Greatness, we must be a servant, a steward, and a sower.

DISCUSSION

? Take a moment and think about how you'd rate yourself on each of the three strands: 0 – never, 1 rarely, 2 sometimes, 3 most/all of the time. For each strand that you rated yourself a 0, 1, or 2, what steps can you take this week to move it (them) closer to a 3. Discuss this with your group.

PRAYER

Father, help me to do greatness – to have the heart of a servant, steward, and sower – all for your Glory. In Jesus name, Amen.

NOTES

NOTES

THE PATH OF A FRIEND
LIFE LESSON: FAITHFULNESS/LOYALTY

THE PATH OF A FRIEND

Part 1: The "THINK" of a Friend

 VIDEO

1 Samuel 18:4
Ecclesiastes 4:9-12 (NLT)
Matthew 18:19,20
2 Samuel 1:25,26

LIFE LESSON: _____Faithfulness_____/LOYALTY

1. THINK _____Alignment_____

HOW TO GET ALIGNED RIGHT

"*When you get with the Right People, in the Right Place, at the Right Time, the Right Things will always happen.*" // **Leadershipology.com**

• Align your heart with what you _____value_____

NOTES

"*For where your treasure is, there your heart will be also.*" // **Matthew 6:21**

- Align your heart with _____ people _____ who value most what you value most.

- Align your heart with people who _____ believe _____ in you.

- Align with people who have your back and your _____ back _____, not just because of what you do, but because of WHO you are.

- Align your heart with people who make your _____ heart _____ better.

🔑 KEY THOUGHTS

A friend **THINKS** alignment. However, most men do not think this way. *Matthew 18:19-20 says, "Again I say to you that if two of you agree on earth concerning anything that they ask, it will be done for them by my Father in heaven. For where two or more of you are gathered in My name, I am there in the midst of them."*

When you get with the right people, in the right place, at the right time, the right things can happen.

NOTES

45

To get aligned right:

- **Align your heart with what you value.** This begins with you knowing what is important to you. Matthew 6:21 says, "For where your treasure is, there your heart will be also." Do not follow your heart. Rather, go with what you treasure. When you decide what is important to you, your heart will follow. Align your heart with what you value.

- **Align your heart with people who value most what you most value.** You must be equally yoked to have great friendships. You need to be doing life with people who value the same things.

- **Align your heart with people who believe in you.** This cannot be overstated. There will always be people in your life who do not believe in you. Why? They do not believe in themselves. The only reason people have a strong believe in themselves is because they have a strong belief in God.

- **Align you heart with people who have your back and heart** – not because of what you do, but because of who you are. Men should not be friends just because they work together, go to church together, or have similar interests. They should have friendships because of who they are striving to be in God … like David who was a man after God's own heart.

- **Align you heart with people who make you and your heart better because of your friendship.**

NOTES

🗨 DISCUSSION

? What are some things you treasure/value?

? Do the men in your life value the same things you value? If not, what can you do to align with men who value what you value?

? Discuss some ways you can show a friend that you believe in them.

? David was a man after the heart of God. How would you describe who you are striving to be in God?

? Are your alignments helping you to be better … because of your friendship?

☝ PRAYER

Lord, help me to Think Alignment … to get in the right place, with the right people, so the right things can happen. In Jesus name, Amen.

NOTES

THE PATH OF A FRIEND

Part 2: The "BE" of a Friend

■ VIDEO

LIFE LESSON: FAITHFULNESS/LOYALTY

1. **THINK ALIGNMENT**

2. **BE** _____Trust_____ **-WORTHY**

3 WAYS TO BE WORTHY OF TRUST

- Love _____God_____ with all your heart. *(Mark 12:28-34)*

- Love your _____neighbor_____ as you love yourself... the way you would like to be loved. *(1 Samuel 20:16,17)*

- Love at all _____times_____. *(Proverbs 17:17, Proverbs 18:24)*

NOTES

KEY THOUGHTS

To be a friend, a man must **BE** trustworthy.

The lives of David and Jonathan provide a biblical model for male friendship. They had the best interest of the other person in mind.

Jonathan was the initiator in the relationship. Don't feel bad if you are the one who initiates in the relationship. At times, you may even feel you are doing more work in the relationship. Just be that guy … always be that guy.

To be faithful, you must be trustworthy. There are three ways to be worthy of trust:

- **Love God with all your heart.** Don't just love God, love God with all you heart. God wants us willingly to love Him, to have relationship with Him. He looks at the heart of a man, as He did with David. Be a man who wants to be in relationship with the Lord, loving Him with all of your heart.

- **Love your friend as you love yourself** … the way you would want someone to love you. Be a friend who brings what you bring. Be all in, knowing friendship is never 50/50. People tend to have a transactional mindset – I'll do this, if you do that. Align with people not based on what you do, but rather on who you are in their life. Then, be "all in."

NOTES

- **Love at all times.** Love your friends whether they are on the mountaintop or in a pit. Seek to be a friend who sticks closer than a brother. Seek to be trustworthy.

The focus of the Path of a Friend is not about how to find a good friend. Rather, it is about how you can become the friend that everybody would want to have.

🗨 DISCUSSION

? Discuss the three ways to be worthy of trust. Which of the three is your strongest? Which one do you need to work on the most and why?

☝ PRAYER

Father, I am so grateful for You. I desire to love you with all my heart and my friends as I do myself. Help me to grow in my relationship with You and to be the kind of friend that loves at all times … one who sticks closer than a brother. Help me to be a man worth of trust and the kind of friend that everybody would want to have. In Jesus name, Amen.

NOTES

THE PATH OF A FRIEND

Part 3: The "DO" of a Friend

🎬 **VIDEO**

1. **THINK ALIGNMENT**

2. **BE TRUST-WORTHY**

3. **DO** _____Covenant_____

LIFE LESSON: FAITHFULNESS/LOYALTY

1 Samuel 18:1,3,4

FIVE COVENANTAL COMMITMENTS OF A RIGHT FRIEND

• Commit to _____Serve_____

• Commit to _____Honor_____

NOTES

> ❝ *Honor is not given because it is deserved by its recipient. It can only be given out of a heart of honor from one who is honorable.*" // **Leadershipology.com**

- Commit to be _____Vulnerable_____ *(1 Samuel 13:19-22)*

- Commit to _____Value_____

- Commit to _____Stay Close_____ *(Proverbs 17:17, Proverbs 18:24)*

What is a FRIEND? by Keith A. Craft
A Friend is…
Someone who loves you, no matter WHAT.
Someone who sticks with you, when you've been STUCK.
Someone who is close only because they want to BE.
Someone who gets in your way, only if you are going down.
Someone who believes in you when you don't believe in yourself.
Someone who SEES the best in you, when your WORST has been displayed.
Someone who SPEAKS more highly of you than you could possibly ever deserve.
Someone who has your best interest in mind even before their own.
Someone who enjoys your company, even when you are SICK of yourself.
Someone who ENCOURAGES you when you have nothing left to GIVE.
Someone with whom you can be yourself and your valued every time you are together.
Someone who appreciates your God given uniqueness.
Someone who makes you feel like the most special person in the world.
Someone who recognizes your GREATNESS and openly benefits from it.

NOTES

54

Someone who gives honor where honor is due.
Someone whose goal is to help you be better, achieve your dreams and who will "Push" you up.
Someone who will listen for the purpose of understanding you better.
Someone who will not have unrealistic expectations.
Someone who is not easily offended, when offense could be taken.
Someone who is not overwhelmed by that which is overwhelming.
Someone who willingly GIVES to you the very BEST they have to give.
This is the kind of friend I wish to have … so, that is the kind of friend I must be.

KEY THOUGHTS

Friends **THINK** Alignment, **BE** Trustworthy, and **DO** Covenant.

1 Samuel 18, "Now when he had finished speaking to Saul, the soul of Jonathan was knit to the soul of David, and Jonathan loved him as his own soul." Saul had turned against David and was kicking him out of the house. Jonathan made a covenant with David because he loved him as his own soul. He took off his robe and he gave it to David, along with his armor, sword, bow, and belt.

Each of these items represented one of the five covenantal or commitments of a "right" friend.

- **Commit to serve** – to do commitment, you must commit to serve. Jonathan gave David his robe. His robe was significant of his stature, his rank, his rightful inheritance. Brotherly friends give up their rank in their relationship because both are there to serve one another, making neither rank higher than the other. It's also a sign of Jonathan saying, "What's mine is yours."

NOTES

_____

_____

_____

_____

_____

_____

- **Commit to honor** – Jonathan gave David his garments. Jonathan was a warrior, he had tremendous military victories. Therefore, his garments represented his merit and honor. By giving them to David, Jonathan was saying, "As my covenant friend, my success and my honor is your success and your honor."

- **Commitment to vulnerability** – Jonathan gave David his sword. This was a sign of his vulnerability as he gave up his defense and his offense, which signified him giving up his right to be right … to be defensive or offended in their relationship. Only Saul and Jonathan had a sword and spear in all of Israel.

- **Commit to value** – Jonathan also gave David his bow, which was his most prized possession. The song of the bow was written about Jonathan's bow while David was mourning Jonathan's death. David ordered that all the children be taught the song. In other words, Jonathan, while making covenant with David, was making the statement that his friendship was more valuable to him than his most prized possession. When we're going to have covenantal friendships, the things in our life have to mean less than the people in our life.

- **Commitment to stay close** - Jonathan gave David his belt, which was what held everything he needed closest to him (so that in any given moment he could reach what he needed most) and gave that to David. Proverbs 17:17 says, "A friend is always loyal, and a brother is born to help in time of need." A man who has friends must show himself friendly, and there is a friend that sticks closer than a brother does.

💬 DISCUSSION

? Knowing the five commitments of a right friend, what spoke most to you?

? Are there changes you need to make in how you approach "right" friendships? Provide an example.

✍ PRAYER

Father, help me to be the "right" kind of friend, a committed friend. Help me to have covenant relationships with a heart committed to serve, honor, be vulnerable, value, and stay close. Help me to be aligned with people because of who they are and who I am ... not because of what we do, as that will be a natural outgrowth of who we are in You. In Jesus name, Amen.

NOTES

NOTES

SESSION 5

THE PATH OF A LOVER
LIFE LESSON: EXCELLENCE

THE PATH OF A LOVER

Part 1: The "THINK" of a Lover

VIDEO

LIFE LESSON: _____ **Excellence** _____

❝*Excellence is a way of practicing according to your potential as if anytime the game of life depends on your last shot.*❞ **// Leadershipology.com**

Matthew 22:36-40
Psalm 18:1-3
Acts 13:22

1. THINK _____ Initiate _____

Matthew 7:12 MSG

NOTES

3 INITIATIVES OF A GREAT LOVER

- Great lovers initiate loving people they love, the way _____ they _____ need to be loved.

- Great lovers initiate _____ forgiveness _____

- Great lovers are great _____ apologizers _____ *(1 Samuel 18:17-29 NKJV)*

THREE REASONS TO INITIATE

- God has called us to be change-agents.

  "*Leaders are Change-Agents that make any change possible." // ***Leadershipology 101**

- Things need to move in the right direction.

  "*Newtons First Law of Motion: When viewed in an inertial reference frame, an object either is at rest or moves at a constant velocity, unless acted upon by an external force.*

- Things need to change for the right reason.

NOTES

63

> "*Being the change you want to see is the most important part of any change you want to see.*" // **Leadershipology.com**

> "*Cynicism is the worst disease a leader can catch! Leaders lead with a spirit of optimism that initiates and provokes positive change!*" // **Leadershipology.com**

KEY THOUGHTS

Great lovers are initiators – they **THINK**, "Initiate."

Being a Great Lover, one who is capable of True Love, begins with being a Great Lover of God.

When men initiate, they give direction, provide security, promote stability, establish expectation, and create order.

Great lovers initiate three things: 1) love – loving people they way they need to be loved; 2) forgiveness – you are forgiven as you forgive; 3) apologies – be quick to apologize.

Great lovers initiate because: 1) God has called us to be change agents; 2) things need to move in the right direction; 3) things need to move for the right reasons. Initiate the right things, for the right reasons to get things moving in the right direction.

Being the change you want to see is the most important part of any change you want to see.

NOTES

🗩 DISCUSSION

Great lovers initiate three things: 1) love; 2) forgiveness; and 3) apologies. Discuss the following:

? Think about a person with whom you want to begin "loving more like they need to be loved." This person may be your wife, a child, a friend, your mother or father, or someone else close to you. What is one thing you can do today to begin loving him/her more like they need to be loved?

? Think about a person with whom you want to forgive. What can you do today to forgive him/her?

? Think about a person with whom you want to extend an apology but have not. What has held you back? What do you need to do to make it happen?

☝ PRAYER

Father, help me to be a man that is a great lover ... one who initiates love, forgiveness, and apologies. I thank you for your love and forgiveness and want to be an example of it. In Jesus name, Amen.

NOTES

_____

_____

_____

_____

_____

_____

_____

THE PATH OF A LOVER

Part 2: The "BE" of a Lover

 VIDEO

LIFE LESSON: EXCELLENCE

1. **THINK INITIATE**

2. **BE IN-**_____Tension_____**-ALL**

> ❝Tension is anything that stretches us beyond our normal limits. Therefore leadership is the dissonance our normal must embrace for greatness." // **Leadershipology.com**

> ❝Conflict is the tension between where we are and where we ought to be." // **Leadershipology.com**

TOP 10 DIVINE TENSIONS

- **Wisdom**

NOTES ——————————————————————————

❝ *Wisdom is the spirit of God that enables us to differentiate not only between good and evil, but good and best; and empowers us to implement the will of God in any and every situation.*" // **Leadershipology.com**

- _____ Knowledge _____

❝ *If knowledge is power then learning is the generator.*" // **Leadershipology.com**

> **TBQ:** "*Knowledge is power' in and of itself is a misnomer. Just because you have knowledge of something does not mean you have power. Knowledge means illumination of the mind. Just because you know about something or someone doesn't mean you have power. You gain power when you use knowledge to make you better. You become better when you learn from what you know about. Your ability to accurately use knowledge is what gives you the power not only to become a better person, but to make anything and everything better because of what you have learned.*"

- **Understanding**

❝ *We lead our heart when we trust in The Lord with ALL of our heart and DO NOT lean to our own understanding which leads to misperceptions.*" // **Leadershipology.com**

NOTES

- <u>   Excellence   </u>

> 66 *Excellence is a commitment to be your best, to do your best…
> that empowers you to see the best in others, and to never allow the
> good to be robber of the best."* // **Leadershipology.com**

- **Generosity**

> 66 *The evidence of a pure heart that is empowered to See God is a heart that sees what
> God does and does what God does best. What does God do best? He gives. He gives His best
> to us. And when we give our best we do what God does best."* // **Leadershipology.com**

- <u>   Forgiveness   </u>

> 66 *Forgiveness is the hardest thing you will ever do, but it is the
> greatest thing you will ever do."* // **Leadershipology.com**

- **Loyalty**

> 66 *Loyalty is doing more than you are asked to do that will gain you
> more FAVOR than you could ever ask."* // **Leadershipology.com**

NOTES

- _____ Positive _____ Attitude

> **❝** *When you view things through the lens of gratitude, you will be empowered to have a positive attitude."* // **Leadershipology.com**

- **Honor**

> **❝** *We don't give honor because someone deserves it. We give honor because we are honorable."* // **Leadershipology.com**

- _____ Marriage _____

> **❝** *Decide to not just be a great man, but a great husband. Because truly, if you are not a great husband, you are not a great man!"* // **Leadershipology.com**

> **❝** *Most of us plateau when we lose the tension between where we are and where we ought to be." - John Gardiner   "The problems we have are often related to the plateaus in our lives. Our marriage plateaus. Our job plateaus. Our life plateaus. Once anything plateaus, if I lose the tension between where I am and where I need to be, I go into decline. Core Values remind me of what is most important. They have the power to propel me into a hope-filled future, because they keep me focused on what is most important about the future. I've learned to identify more than one strategy for getting to a goal. But the most important stratagem I have learned is that Core*

NOTES

Values make goal achievement possible. Once I know what matters most, I can then set goals to achieve the outcome I want." // **Your Divine Fingerprint, P.88-89**

When the tension seems overwhelming, encourage yourself in the Lord.

1 Samuel 30:1-6 KJV

KEY THOUGHTS

Great lovers are intentional – they **BE**, "In-tension-all." Be in tension about everything … be in-tension-all.

Tension *is anything that stretches us beyond our normal limits.* Therefore, leadership is the dissonance our "normal" must embrace in order for us to realize the "greatness" we each have.

Conflict *is the tension between where we are and where we ought to be.* As men who are lovers, in order for our love to be "true love" and not just "part-time love," we need to be intentional about certain areas that "in love" will be in-tension-all the time.

Revisit the list of Divine Tensions above. Tension arises with each of these when we intentionally move from talking about them to living them.

We plateau when we lost the tension between where we are and where we ought to be. When we settle by saying, "Oh, I am okay." At that very moment, the tension disappears.

NOTES

In encouraging yourself, remember why you chose to embrace excellence, why you got married, why you honor others, why you value having a positive attitude, etc. Embrace those tensions – embrace Wisdom, choosing best over good. Be in-tension-all about everything.

DISCUSSION

? What is something you have not been in-tension-all about but want to begin? What can do today to begin being in-tension-all about it?

? When the tension seems overwhelming, how do you encourage yourself? Does this include encouraging yourself in the Lord? How do you do that?

? Based on the list of tensions above, pick one talk about some of the reasons "why" you choose to embrace it and the excellence it requires.

PRAYER

Father, please give me the strength to be in-tension-all – to embrace divine tensions, to be in-tension-all about everything. When the tension seems overwhelming, I encourage myself in You Lord, as Your Word says I can do all things in Christ who strengthens me. In Jesus name, Amen.

NOTES

NOTES

THE PATH OF A LOVER

Part 3: The "DO" of a Lover

▤ VIDEO

1. **THINK INITIATE**

2. **BE IN-TENSION-ALL**

3. **DO YOUR** _____Best_____

LIFE LESSON: EXCELLENCE

❝ *To be able to Do your Best, you have to choose to Be your Best. To choose to Be your Best, you have to THINK, 'I want the BEST!'"* // **Leadershipology.com**

❝ *Anybody worth you loving, is worth you giving them nothing less than you best!"* // **Leadershipology.com**

Psalm 119:7-18, 29-41

NOTES

TWO WAYS TO DO YOUR BEST

Practice _____Generosity_____

" *When we are generous, we are the most like God." //* **Leadershipology.com**

> **TBQ:** *Generosity is fully expressed when you give your best. That is what God did when He gave His only Son Jesus. Being a generous person is not about possessing a certain personality, characteristic, or having more than others. It's about giving the best YOU have out of a heart of love. When you are generous with your time, talent and your treasure, then and only then can you discover what it is to be truly God-like.*

Be ___ALL___ ___IN___

"All in…" by Keith A. Craft
"All In…"what does it mean?
Two small words, but essential to a dream.
You can talk "All in…"or you can BE "All in…"
But one thing is for sure, there's only one way you can win.

"All in…"is more than theoretical.
You can talk it, you can say it and even sound poetical.
But "All in…" means, just what it means.
Being "All in…"makes a dream, THE dream.

You can't be "All in…"and BE by yourself.
It takes more than you, to get a dream off the shelf.
You have to have people, that you invest yourself in.
You see your not "All in…" without people, you need people to win.

"All in…" is about you, being the best you, you can BE.
It's not about you if it's "what's in it for me?"
It's about sacrificing, what you thought "IT" would be.
By BEING "All in…"you discover your true "Me!"

Some people talk it and they jump in with both feet.
But they soon feel the weight and the weight makes them feel "incomplete."
A fear comes over them, as to what "All in..." might cost.
They begin to doubt and fear about what could be lost.

"All in..." will awaken the strong and reveal the weak.
It will introduce you to yourself, what your not and what you seek.
Until you are "All in..." you will never know the depth.
Of what you have IN you, that you didn't know you had left.

"All in..." is a commitment to "go-there" where you've never been.
It's about the right people in the right places doing the right things to win.
"All in..." what does it mean?
It's doing whatever it takes to make a dream...THE dream!

So in the end, don't talk "All In..." BE "All in...!"
Don't just start the race, it's never too late to Be what you could have been.
You've got what it takes, but there's only one way to know.
Jump "All in..." and you'll make everything grow!

NOTES

KEY THOUGHTS

Great lovers **DO** their best.

David gave his best to his father, his king, and God.

Great lovers give God their best. As Pastor Keith said to Pastor Sheila, "You be your best for God and I'll be my best. Together, we give God our best."

Giving God your best is what the First Fruit is all about. It is not about being the First, but it is about the First being the Best.

We are men. We are lovers. We do our best not because of what we get out of it but because that is the way we roll in our role. Do your best at your job, with your wife, with your kids … and with anything and everything you choose to do in life, do your best.

Your best today will not be your best tomorrow. So do not feel bad about knowing today what you could have done yesterday. Do your best today, as God will be your rewarder.

DISCUSSION

? To what or whom in your life do you need to begin giving your best?

NOTES

? What will you do to begin giving him/her/it your best?

? What drives you to want to do your best?

☝ PRAYER

Father, I want to give You my best. I know it is not about being the best but doing my best. Please forgive me where I have fallen short, as my heart is to do all I do as unto you, that I may live and keep your Word. Help me to grow and develop into the best me I can be ... at my job, with my wife and kids, and with anything and everything I do in life.

NOTES

NOTES

SESSION 6

THE PATH OF A WARRIOR
LIFE LESSON: FIGHT/CONFLICT RESOLUTION

SESSION 6
THE PATH OF A WARRIOR

Part 1: The "THINK" of a Warrior

▸ VIDEO

Acts 13:21-23 NLT
1 Samuel 16:1-13 NLT

1. **THINK** _____Worship_____

1 Samuel 16:14-23 NLT

LIFE LESSON: FIGHT/CONFLICT RESOLUTION

GOD IS LOOKING FOR MEN WHOSE HEARTS:

- _____Value_____ what He values *(Psalm 40:1-11)*

- Are _____confident_____ in the Lord's goodness *(Psalm 27:1-11, 13 NLT)*

NOTES

84

🔑 KEY THOUGHTS

Warriors **THINK** Worship.

The Lord does not see as man sees; for a man looks at the outward appearance, but the Lord looks at the heart. He looks for men whose hearts value what He values.

David had the ability through his worship to run off distressing spirits ... that's what a warrior does.

Even when a true warrior is in a pit, he worships. By worshiping even under duress the Bible says others see it and give praise to God because the warrior was faithful in worship even in the midst of struggle.

Warriors declare God's faithfulness, salvation, loving-kindness, and truth in the assembly and are confident in His goodness.

Warriors learn to worship. You do not have to be a great signer. Lift your hands and lead the way. Know that the assembly is watching ... people will respond because you worship.

Warriors Think Worship ... that is how David thought and that is why God said that he was a man after My own heart.

NOTES

💬 DISCUSSION

? When King Saul was looking for someone to play the harp to ease his distress, reports about David reached him. David had distinguished himself and was known for his ability to worship. He was faithful in worshiping and as a result his name was the first to reach the ears of King Saul. What can we do in our own lives to be found faithful in honoring and worshiping God?

? What can we do outside of a church service to worship the Lord?

? Even when a warrior is in a pit, he STILL worships and as a result others are drawn to God. How can we strengthen our resolve, refocus our attention in the midst of trouble, and declare the faithfulness, loving-kindness, truth, and salvation of God? What are some practical steps we can take today?

? Warriors are confident in the Lord's goodness! What are some daily disciplines you can start today that keep God's faithfulness and goodness at the forefront of our thinking? Gratitude journal? Setting an alarm on your phone to remind you to stop in the middle of your day and praise/ give thanks to God?

NOTES

☝ PRAYER

Father, I give myself to you. I deeply desire to worship You, in reverence and awe. Even in times when I am feeling down, my desire is to worship You, to magnify You, to glorify You. Please guide me as I strive to develop a lifestyle of worship. Help me to be a Warrior that Thinks worship … like David … a man after Your own heart. In Jesus name, Amen.

NOTES

THE PATH OF A WARRIOR

Part 2: The "BE" of a Warrior

🎬 **VIDEO**

LIFE LESSON: FIGHT/CONFLICT RESOLUTION

1. **THINK WORSHIP**

2. **BE A** _____Mighty_____ **MAN**

Joel 3:9,10; 2 Samuel 23:8-17; Proverbs 28:1

MIGHTY MAN ARE BOLD

- Mighty Men are **B**_____rave_____ *(1 Tim. 6:12; 2 Tim. 4:7)*

- Mighty Men **O**_____vercome_____ *(Revelation 2:26; 3:5, 12, 21; 21:7)*

- Mighty Men **L**_____ive_____ with a Transcendent Cause *(Colossians 3:17, 23, 24)*

- Mighty Men **D**_____iscipline_____ themselves *(2 Timothy 1:7)*

NOTES

🗝 **KEY THOUGHTS**

Warriors **THINK** Worship and **BE** a Mighty Man.

A Mighty Men is BOLD. We have to be willing, according to Joel 3, to be awakened. Let's be awakened to this spirit of a Mighty Man. Why? Because until we put life in the context of war, we will misunderstand 90 percent of what is happening. When you are having problems in your marriage, when you are having problems on your job, when you are having problems in your life, and/or having problems with yourself, remember this … it is in the context of war.

There is a real war that's going on, a war for your soul, a war for your marriage, a war for your children, a war for your ability to be a producer in the Kingdom of God. The righteous are as bold as a lion. We must decide to be brave. Brave doesn't mean you don't ever feel fear. Bravery means you face your fear. You take action regardless of the fear that you feel.

Then we overcome. We choose to be overcomers. Why? With the words that we say, with the blood of the Lamb that has washed us, that has cleansed us. We choose to live with a transcendent cause, to do everything unto the Lord, and to discipline ourselves. We have been given a spirit of power, a spirit of love, and a spirit of sound mind, self-discipline.

NOTES

💬 DISCUSSION

? Have you identified your transcendent cause? The WHY behind the WHAT of everything you do?

? How can you put your job or vocation in the context of your transcendent cause? Your marriage? Your children?

? What is one area of your life where you will choose today to increase the level of discipline? What are some practical steps you will put in place to make this happen? Who will you be accountable to in this new discipline?

☝ PRAYER

Father, I answer the call to be a Mighty Man who lives with a transcendent cause. Help me to be brave and to face my fears for I know with You on my side whom shall I fear. Help me to be an overcomer, to do all I do as unto you, to be disciplined. Thank you for giving me a spirit of power, love, and of a sound mind. In Jesus name, Amen.

NOTES

THE PATH OF A WARRIOR

Part 3: The "DO" of a Warrior

🎬 VIDEO

1. **THINK WORSHIP**

2. **BE A MIGHTY MAN**

3. **DO** _____Conquer_____

LIFE LESSON: FIGHT/CONFLICT RESOLUTION

1 Samuel 17:11,45-47 NLT
Psalm 18:30-39 NLT

🔑 KEY THOUGHTS

Warriors **DO** Conquer.

A Warrior's destiny … your destiny, is to conquer. It does not matter the giant. It does not matter the situation. It does not matter the circumstances. In your life, as a warrior, **DO** conquer. That's God's destiny.

NOTES

To "DO" Conquer first you have to hear right. The Israelite army hears the threats of a giant. What they heard paralyzed them with fear. David, on the other hand, heard an "uncircumcised Philistine" cursing his God and he heard the promise of what would be done for the man that defeated him. What he heard empowered him.

Warriors understand who the battle really belongs to. God this is your fight. No matter what the enemy is, I will not be afraid. God is for me so who can be against me.

Warriors understand who the victory really belongs to. The victory is for Him and to prove to everybody else it is truly God. If he can help you, He can help anybody.

🗨 DISCUSSION

The entire Israelite army "KNEW" Goliath was too big to defeat and they HEARD the threats of what could happen to them for the negative. Pastor Keith pointed out that fear is a spirit. What has been an enemy in your life where you now recognize that fear has held you back?

? What can you do to turn the battle over to the Lord and HEAR the promises of God so that you are empowered to conquer your enemy?

? How can you set a monument, create a remembrance, or build an altar to God's glory and honor for winning the battles in your life so that it becomes a lasting legacy for those that follow you and for your children?

NOTES

☝ PRAYER

Father, I thank you the battle is not mine but yours and every victory is not mine, but is yours. Your way is perfect and your promises prove true. You give me strength and make my way perfect. I thank you that I am the head and not the tail, first and not last. I thank you that you have BIG plans for me. Father, I will not stop until I conquer, fighting every battle all for your glory! In Jesus name, Amen.

NOTES

NOTES

SESSION 7

THE PATH OF A KING

LIFE LESSON: RULE

THE PATH OF A KING

Part 1: The "THINK" of a King

▶ VIDEO

Revelation 1:1-6

LIFE LESSON:	Rule

Genesis 1:26-28

1. **THINK** _____Kingdom_____

1 Chronicles 29:10-19 NLT
Matthew 6:9-13

THINK KINGDOM

• The kingdom is _____to_____ us…"He loved us"

NOTES

- The kingdom is _____in_____ us…"He washed us"

- The kingdom is _____through_____ us…"He made us to be Kings and Priests

- The kingdom of God functions by a _____revelation_____ of Jesus Christ for our example to follow.

🔑 KEY THOUGHTS

Kings **THINK**, "Kingdom."

The Bible says to seek first the Kingdom of God and His righteousness (His right way of doing things) and all these other things will be added unto you. It is our job on the path of a King to think Kingdom.

God's Kingdom works like this … "For Yours is the kingdom, and the power, and the glory, forever. Amen." It is forever … God is saying he must have Kings and he must have Priests. As a man, you must get the revelation on which one of these you are. Once you do, you will operate in that function.

As a king, you are to operate on the earth as a businessman, a king in the house of God, a king in the Kingdom of God for the purpose of living with a transcendent cause. When we live with a transcendent cause, God is giving us kingdoms to advance His kingdom. It is not about our kingdoms – career, money, life, and so on. Rather, everything is about Him and advancing His Kingdom, for His glory.

NOTES

101

🗩 DISCUSSION

? What does it mean to have a Kingdom mindset? Do you have one?

? What are some things that have gotten in the way of you thinking Kingdom and living with a transcendent cause?

☝ PRAYER

Lord, thank you for being a God of structure and for having a role for me to play in you plan. Help me to Think Kingdom in all I do and to step into and fully embrace the role you have called me to play. I know that life is not about my kingdoms, such as my career, money, and life … rather, everything is about You and advancing your Kingdom, for Your glory. In Jesus name, Amen.

NOTES

NOTES

THE PATH OF A KING

Part 2: The "BE" of a King

▶ VIDEO

1. **THINK KINGDOM**

2. **BE** _____Powerful_____

   • Know you are _____called_____

> Ephesians 4:1
> 1 Thessalonians 2:12
> 1 Peter 2:9, 10

   • _____Answer_____ the call as a Priest or a King

> *(1 Samuel 3:1-10, 19-21, 1 Samuel 9:1-19, 10:1)*

LIFE LESSON: RULE

NOTES

🔑 <u>KEY THOUGHTS</u>

Kings **BE** "Powerful."

You are a true disciple when you do what Jesus would do, not what you would do. In that context, Jesus' disciples asked Him how to pray and He shared the Lord's Prayer. He ended it by saying, "For thine is the Kingdom, and the power, and the glory, forever. Amen." As men on the path of a king, we have to Think Kingdom and Be Powerful.

First, you must know that you are Called ... that God has called you into His Kingdom. You are not just called to make your dream come true or use your gifts. You are called into the Kingdom. When you understand this, God gives you a priest.

Kings and Priests flow together to advance the Kingdom of God. A true priest is one who sees things in life that can help you and is anointed to speak the Word of God over your life.

Second, you must answer the call. On the path of a king, know that you are powerful. You power is attached to the priest with whom God aligns you. Just as when Saul was looking for donkeys for his dad, God had a different plan. Many people are looking for donkeys and have not yet found their priest. When they do, they go from looking for donkeys to being a king.

NOTES

💬 DISCUSSION

? What does it mean to know you are called … that God has called you into His Kingdom?

? Do you know the role God has called you to play – King or Priest?

? Have you answered your call? If not, step can you take to do so? If so, what is one thing can you do immediately to add more value to the King/Priest relationship you have?

☝ PRAYER

Father, I thank you that you have called me to play a key role in advancing your Kingdom. I pray that as I step into this role you would guide me and that I would function in that role, according to your will. In Jesus name, Amen.

NOTES

NOTES

SESSION 7
THE PATH OF A KING

Part 3: The "DO" of a King

🎬 **VIDEO**

1. **THINK KINGDOM**

2. **BE POWERFUL**

3. **DO** _____ Glory _____

LIFE LESSON: RULE

Deuteronomy 20:1-4

KINGDOM FUNCTION OF PRIESTS

- Proclaim _____ The Good _____ News

- Cast _____ Vision _____

- Declare _____ Blessing _____

NOTES

KINGDOM FUNCTION OF KINGS

- Take _____ Dominion _____

- Bring _____ Provision _____

- Establish _____ Order _____

DISCOVER, DEVELOP, DEPLOY

Deploy
Together
_____

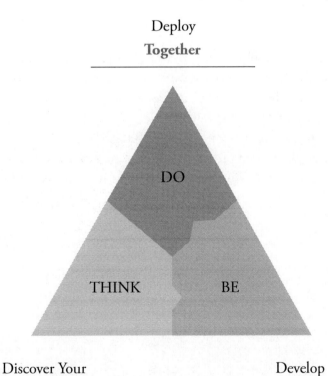

DO

THINK   BE

Discover Your   Develop
Calling   **Yourself**
_____   _____

🔑 KEY THOUGHTS

Kings **DO** Glory.

We Do Glory when we know our calling and function on earth in that calling. Your highest purpose in life is to function in your call with whom God has called you to align. God's number one goal is to establish His kingdom in the earth.

The Kingdom function of Priests is to proclaim the Good News, cast vision and declare blessing.

The Kingdom function of Kings is to take dominion, bring provision, and establish order. True Kings are aligned with their Priest. They live with a transcendent cause. They are the financial leaders in the Kingdom of God who like David set their affection…their passion on the House of God and make it their life long goal to advance God's Kingdom in the earth with all their financial might!

Discover your calling, Develop yourself, and Deploy together. As a king, discover your calling. Develop yourself in that calling. In other words, you've got to be the one that Thinks Kingdom. You've got to be the one that chooses to Be Powerful. You've got to be the one that chooses to Do Glory. Then deploy together. Get aligned not just in a good church, but get aligned with a priest. Again, this is foreign to many people's thinking. That's why we are doing this Bible Study … God's made us to be kings and priests. He did not make us to be Christian men in the church. He made us to function in the Kingdom. He loved us, washed us, and made us to be kings and priests. That is in the book of Revelation. Some may say, "Well, isn't that Old Testament?" Well,

NOTES

if the Old Testament is in Revelation, and it is, the Old Testament is revealed. It is like everything coming together to say this is how My Kingdom works.

💬 DISCUSSION

? What spoke most to you in this segment?

? What does it mean to take dominion ... to bring provision to the House ... to bring order?

? How can you begin to fully function in each?

☝ PRAYER

Father, it is such an honor to be a part of what you are doing. I know my calling and deeply desire to function in it ... not by myself but with whom you have called me to function. God your number one goal is to establish Your kingdom in the earth. Guide me as I do my part to bring You glory. In Jesus name, Amen.

NOTES

NOTES ———

SESSION 8

THE PATH OF A FATHER
LIFE LESSON: LEGACY

THE PATH OF A FATHER

Part 1: The "THINK" of a Father

📽 **VIDEO**

LIFE LESSON: _____

1. **THE PATH OF A** _____Son_____ **LIFE LESSON:** _____Honor_____

2. **THE PATH OF A** _____Servant_____ **LIFE LESSON:** _____Fellowship that breeds leadership_____

3. **THE PATH OF A** _____Friend_____ **LIFE LESSON:** _____Faithfulness/Loyalty_____

4. **THE PATH OF A** _____Lover_____ **LIFE LESSON:** _____Excellence_____

5. **THE PATH OF A** _____Warrior_____ **LIFE LESSON:** _____Fight/Conflict Resolution_____

6. **THE PATH OF A** _____King_____ **LIFE LESSON:** _____Rule_____

7. **THE PATH OF A** _____Father_____ **LIFE LESSON:** _____Legacy_____

NOTES

1. **THINK GROW YOUR** _____Leadership_____ **... SO YOU ARE QUALIFIED TO LEAD OTHERS.**

> 66 *Leadership is the capacity of an individual to discover their passion, develop their vision and deploy their greatness that elevates them personally and creates the ability to empower others to do the same."* // **Leadershipology.com**

WAYS TO GROW YOUR LEADERSHIP

- Honor the Lord by living a _____God_____-_____First_____ life *(Exodus 13:13,14, Proverbs 3:5-10)*

> 66 *The greatest legacy a father can leave his children is that he put God first with his time, his talent, and his treasure."* // **Leadershipology.com**

- Rule your spirit, by walking in the Spirit *(Proverbs 16:32; 25:28; 29:2, Galatians 5:13-25)*

> 66 *The job of a father is to lead himself to give honor to the heavenly Father and lead his family with follow-able excellence."* // **Leadershipology.com**

- Find a need and _____Lead_____ it *(Psalm 78:70-72)*

NOTES

> *"If you are too big to follow, you are too small to lead."* // **Leadershipology.com**

> *"Servant-leadership is your gateway to greatness."* // **Your Divine Fingerprint, p.113**

KEY THOUGHTS

Quick review. The path of a son is to learn Honor. The path of a servant is to learn Followship. The path of a friend is to learn Faithfulness. The path of a lover is to learn Excellence. The path of a warrior is to learn Conflict Resolution (how to fight the good fight and to fight right). The path of a king is to learn how to Rule. The path of a father is to leave a Legacy (and to know how to leave a legacy).

Fathers **THINK** Grow your Leadership.

Thinking "Grow Your Leadership" is important for you to be qualified to lead others. To be able to think legacy in terms of learning, you must ask yourself, "What and how do I need to … if I am going to leave a legacy?" So how does Thinking Legacy make me think? It makes me think I have got to grow myself so that I'm qualified to lead other people.

In the context of a father, there are ways that you can grow your leadership. First, honor the Lord by living a God-first life. The greatest legacy you can leave your family is to honor the Lord by living a God first life. Second, rule your spirit. You rule your spirit by walking in the spirit – *Proverbs 16:32; 25:28; 29:2* provide a few examples. If you cannot rule your spirit, your kids, employees, and/or friends, will never respect you. Third, find a need and lead it. Servant leadership is the gateway to greatness – revisit *Psalm 78:70-72*.

NOTES

If you are going to leave a legacy, you must live the legacy.

💬 DISCUSSION

? How do you grow your leadership … what are the three ways covered in this segment?

? What does it mean to live a God-first life? How do you do it?

? What does it mean to rule your spirit? How do you rule your spirit? How do you manage your anger? How do you manage your emotions?

? What does it mean to be a servant leader? Are there some areas in your life where you do not have a servant leader mindset? What can you do to be a servant leader in all areas of your life?

☝ PRAYER

Father, I thank you that you created me in your image and according to your likeness. I am grateful you created me to lead and I want to live the legacy you want me to leave. Please help me to grow in my leadership capacity – by putting you first in all I do, ruling my spirit, and having the heart and mind of a servant leader – all for your glory. In Jesus name, Amen.

NOTES

THE PATH OF A FATHER

Part 2: The "BE" of a Father

🎬 VIDEO

1. **THINK GROW YOUR LEADERSHIP**

2. **BE A** _____God_____ **-FATHER**

> ❝*A man's greatest privilege is not being male; his highest honor is not found in the eyes of friends or foes; his most notable achievements cannot be measured by material wealth; but a man's greatest privilege given to him by God is when he becomes a father.*❞
> **// Leadershipology.com**

LIFE LESSON: LEGACY

1 Kings 2:1-4

BE A GOD-FATHER

• God-fathers speak _____strength_____

NOTES

❝*Life doesn't come with an instruction manual, that's why we need fathers.*"
// Leadershipology.com

- God-fathers inspire _____ champions _____

❝*The lessons of Fatherhood are: Unconditional love, serving, tenderness, quality time, mercy, generosity, forgiveness, standards & Leadership!*" **// Leadershipology.com**

- God-fathers have the power to bestow blessing, _____ success _____ and prosperity.

❝*God gives every man who becomes a father, the power to BE a father like Him.*"
// Leadershipology.com

❝*Energy Producers are people who speak BLESSING over people's lives and ENCOURAGE them by proclaiming who they are in God.*" **// Leadershipology.com**

KEY THOUGHTS

BE a God-Father.

A man's greatest privilege is not being a male. His highest honor is not found in the eyes his friends or foes. His notable achievements cannot be measured by material wealth, but a man's greatest privilege is given to him by God … and that's when he becomes a father. Pastor Keith

NOTES

shared that one of his greatest privileges in life is to be a father – both an earthly father and a spiritual father … a God-father.

God-fathers speak strength. That's what they do. Be in a position, even if it's in your last breath, to Be a God-father by speaking strength. Speak strength. No matter how old your children are, no matter the people in your life, when you know that you have a father spirit, speak like it.

God-fathers inspire champions. Pastor Keith shared that from the day his son was born, he has called him, "Champion." He says, "Josh, you're the champion of champions. Be a champion." One time Josh asked, "Dad, why do you call me a champion?" Pastor Keith replied, "Because that's how I see you." "But I haven't won anything, Dad." Speaking as a God-father, Pastor Keith said, "That doesn't matter … I see you as a champion." God-fathers inspire champions. They see everybody in their life as a champion, and they speak that over them.

The lessons of fatherhood are unconditional love, serving, tenderness, quality time, mercy, generosity, forgiveness, standards, and leadership. God-fathers unconditionally love. That does not mean you approve of everything kids do. You still have to draw boundary lines. You serve them. You are tender with them. You give them quality time. You give them mercy. Again, not making them codependent on you, but you give mercy. You are generous. You forgive. You set standards. You give leadership. The standards you set drive the mercy and generosity that you have. Pastor Keith shared that he is not generous with his kids just because they are his kids. Rather, he made decisions along the way … when they are making right decisions, they get the hand of blessing. They always have unconditional love, but they do not get his money if they are not putting God first. Revisit the video segment for more details.

NOTES

God-fathers have the power to bestow blessing, success, and power. God gives every man who becomes a father to be a father like Him. If they choose to go another way (in the context of the Prodigal Son) and they do not value what the Father values, they do not get the value from the father. They get love. They get unconditional forgiveness, but that is only if they have repented. They get mercy, but that is only if they want mercy. They get generosity, but that is only if they are willing to come back from the pigsty and put the robe of the father back on, put the ring back on, and put the sandals back on.

Energy producers are people who speak blessing over people's lives and encourage them by proclaiming who they are in God. That's what God fathers do.

DISCUSSION

? Is it important when speaking strength, you do so no matter who you are speaking with? Why?

? How have you inspired a champion in the past? Are there times you had the opportunity to inspire a champion but did not take it? What held you back?

? How do you give mercy and set standards? How do you be generous and set standards?

NOTES

? Have you spoken a blessing over the people in your lives, encouraging them in who they are in God? Who is someone today you can bless and encourage? Share what you might say to them.

? What is one thing you can do today to not just be a father, but step into being a God-father?

☝ <u>PRAYER</u>

Father, I am so thankful for the insights I am receiving. As I grow into Being a God-father, please help me to boldly and confidently speak strength, inspire champions, and bestow blessing, success, and prosperity over people with whom that I come into contact. Show me Your way Lord ... how You want me to roll in my role as a God-father, for Your glory. In Jesus name, Amen.

NOTES

SESSION 8
THE PATH OF A FATHER

Part 3: The "DO" of a Father

 VIDEO

1. **THINK GROW YOUR LEADERSHIP**

2. **BE A GOD-FATHER**

3. **DO** _____Inheritance_____

LIFE LESSON: LEGACY

1 Chronicles 29:23-28 NLT
1 Peter 1:3-5

" *Live the legacy you want to leave!"* // **Leadershipology.com**

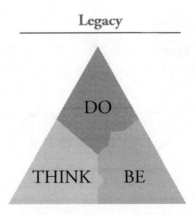

Legacy

DO

THINK   BE

Grow   Model

HOW TO LEAVE A WINNING FATHER'S LEGACY

- Worshiper *(Psalm 5:7, Colossians 1:12)*

- Wisdom: <u>ask the right questions</u> *(Proverbs 8:17-21, James 1:5, Proverbs 18:22, Proverbs13:20)*

- Wellness *(Proverbs 25:12-13, 3 John 1:2)*

- <u>Wealth</u> *(Proverbs 13:22, Matthew 25:14-30, 31-46)*

- <u>Warrior</u>

KEY THOUGHTS

Fathers **DO** Inheritance.

Fathers live the kind of legacy they want to leave.

Live your life in a way that your kids say, like Solomon, said, "I want to be like my father David. What David had on his life, I want to have that on my life, and I want it to be in an even greater measure."

The triad of Legacy Living … "Grow" to the left … "Model" to the right … "Legacy" to the top. If I grow, then I can model and will be able to leave a legacy. In a very simple thought process. If

NOTES

128

I grow in my fathering … model being a God-father … I will leave a legacy.

Revisit "How to Leave a Winning Father's Legacy" shown above. Worshiper, Wisdom, Wellness, Wealth, Warrior. Living these now, so you can leave them tomorrow, is how we Do Inheritance.

🗨 DISCUSSION

? Discuss the list of items in the "How to Leave a Winning Father's Legacy." Spending a few minutes on each, share what does it mean to you and what can you do personally to: 1) Grow in it and 2) Model it?

☝ PRAYER

Father, thank you for giving me eyes to see, ears to hear, and a heart to receive this message. Help me to leave a "Winning Father's Legacy" – to grow where I need to grow and model what needs to be modeled, so that I DO leave an Inheritance – a legacy for Your glory. In Jesus name, Amen.

NOTES

129

SESSIONS VIDEO LINK

HTTP://VIMEO.COM/SHOWCASE/POEM

CONNECT WITH KEITH CRAFT

KEITHCRAFT.COM

Made in the USA
Las Vegas, NV
01 December 2024